THE OXFORD BOOK OF Wedding Music

Thirty Pieces for Organ

Music Department
OXFORD UNIVERSITY PRESS
Oxford and New York

Oxford University Press, Walton Street, Oxford OX2 6DP, England
Oxford University Press, 200 Madison Avenue, New York, NY 10016, USA

Oxford is a trade mark of Oxford University Press

3 5 7 9 10 8 6 4

Printed in Great Britain
on acid-free paper by
St Edmundsbury Press Ltd.,
Bury St Edmunds, Suffolk

CONTENTS

PREFACE

What is it that makes certain pieces enduringly popular at weddings? Given the nature of the occasion, they must be tuneful, accessible, extrovert, and—most importantly—have a clearly defined rhythmic and melodic character that makes an immediate impression in the first few bars. Hence the long-standing popularity of Bach and Handel, trumpet tunes, and marches of all kinds.

This anthology makes no attempts to be a comprehensive repository of every piece that one could ever play, or might be asked for, at a wedding. Clearly such a task would be impossible: all sorts of music can be used for this purpose, and all organists have tried and trusted personal favourites that are off the beaten track. The purpose of this volume is to bring under a single cover the small but select group of pieces to which couples—and organists—return again and again, and which have stood the test of time.

We make no apologies for a general emphasis on the traditional, or even for a similarity in tone of some of the music here—weddings are traditional occasions, and the lasting popularity of these pieces reflects this. A small exception has been made, however, in the inclusion of two new pieces by William Mathias and Andrew Carter, which seemed to fulfil the criteria above whilst striking a lighter and more contemporary note of their own.

For practical purposes, this anthology is loosely arranged in three sections. The first contains quieter music, for use pre-service or during the signing of the register. The second contains music for the entrance of the bride: the favourite marches and trumpet tunes that are short enough for this purpose. Where possible, optional cuts are suggested, and organists should feel free to find their own practical solutions if there are problems of length. The third section contains concluding processional music; some of these pieces are more extended, and obviously all the pieces in the second section suit this purpose equally well.

A number of new arrangements have been specially commissioned for this volume, and existing ones have been updated where appropriate. All the pieces can be played on an organ with two manuals and pedals, and whilst items such as Widor's *Toccata* are limited to a small number of players, much of the material here is only intermediate in difficulty. Registration indications have generally been kept to a minimum, and are suggestions only, to be adapted to the requirements of individual instruments.

Finally, an oft-neglected fact: with two very obvious exceptions, all these pieces can be widely used—and will be extremely popular—at all sorts of occasions other than weddings.

Air

(from Suite No. 3)

J. S. BACH
arr. Gordon Phillips

tr

tr

Sanctify us by thy Goodness

(from Cantata No. 22)

J. S. BACH
arr. P. K.

Jesu, Joy of Man's Desiring

(from Cantata No. 147)

I 8'
II 8' 4' $2\frac{2}{3}$'
III 8' 4'
Ped. 16' 8'

J. S. BACH
arr. P. K.

The arrangement can equally effectively be played on two manuals throughout, with the chorale passages played on I. Small notes are optional and can be omitted; the arrangement can be further simplified by leaving out the chorale harmony and playing the melody only, an octave lower than notated here.

II
III
R.H.
I
III

III
I
III
I
III

I
III
B
A
I

Sheep may Safely Graze

(from Cantata No. 208)

I Flute
II Accompaniment
III Solo Stop

J. S. BACH
arr. Stainton de B. Taylor

I
II
I
tr
tr
II

2
Fine
1
II
III
I
II

II
III
I
II
D.C. al Fine

Prière à Notre-Dame

(from *Suite Gothique*)

Récit [Sw.] Gambe et Voix céleste
Gd. Orgue [Gt.] Flûte ou Bourdon 8'
Pédale Basses douces 8', 16'

L. BOËLLMANN

pp
mf
p
pp
sf
Animato
G.R.
mf

cresc.
f
R.
rit. poco

- - - a poco
1er tempo
R.
dim.
pp
dim.
G.
pp

Ave Maria

I Solo
II Light 8' 4'
Ped. Soft 16' 8'

BACH / GOUNOD
arr. Christopher Morris

A

cresc.

dim.
poco rall.

Aria

(from Concerto Grosso No. 12)

G. F. HANDEL
arr. C. H. Trevor

Some of the quavers may be lightly dotted (♪. ♬) if preferred. The original is in E major.

tr
tr
II
I
II
non legato
rall.
tr

Air

(from *Water Music*)

G. F. HANDEL
arr. Christopher Morris

tr
tr
tr
I - II
tr
tr

I – II

tr

tr
tr

Minuet

(from *Berenice*)

G. F. HANDEL
arr. Patrick Williams

tr
I
mf
f

Solo
mf
II
tr
1
II
p
tr
2
I
f
rall.
tr

Greensleeves

(adapted from an old air)

R. VAUGHAN WILLIAMS
arr. Stanley Roper
ed. Christopher Morris

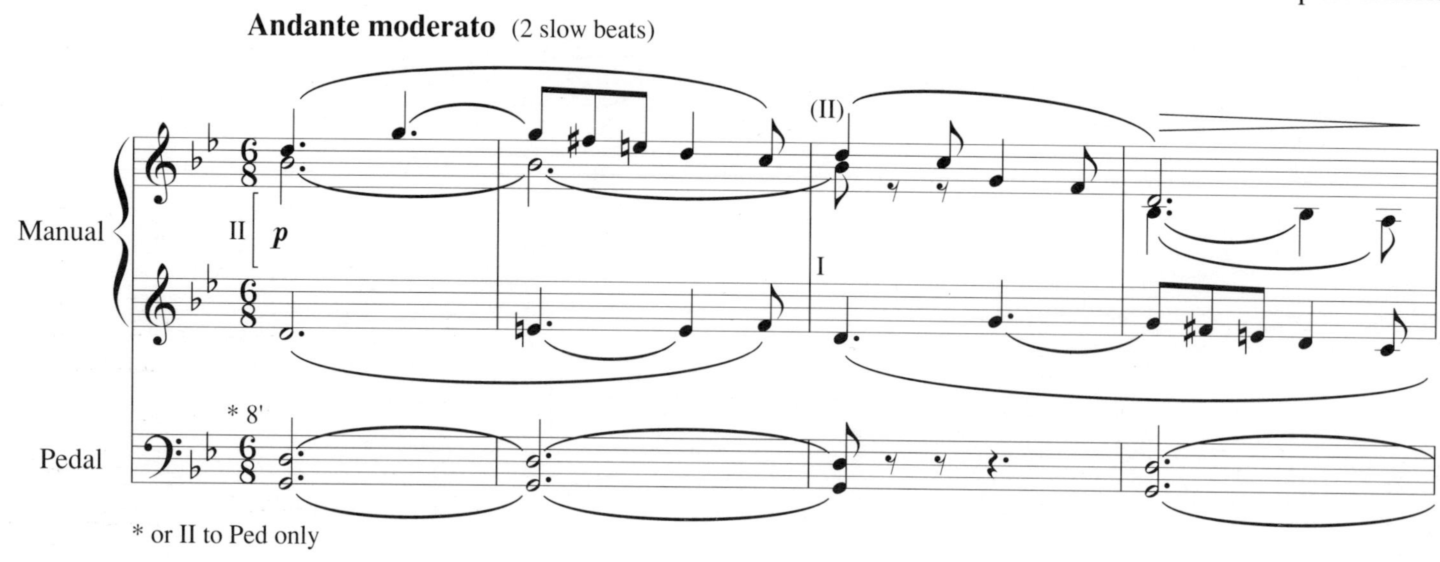

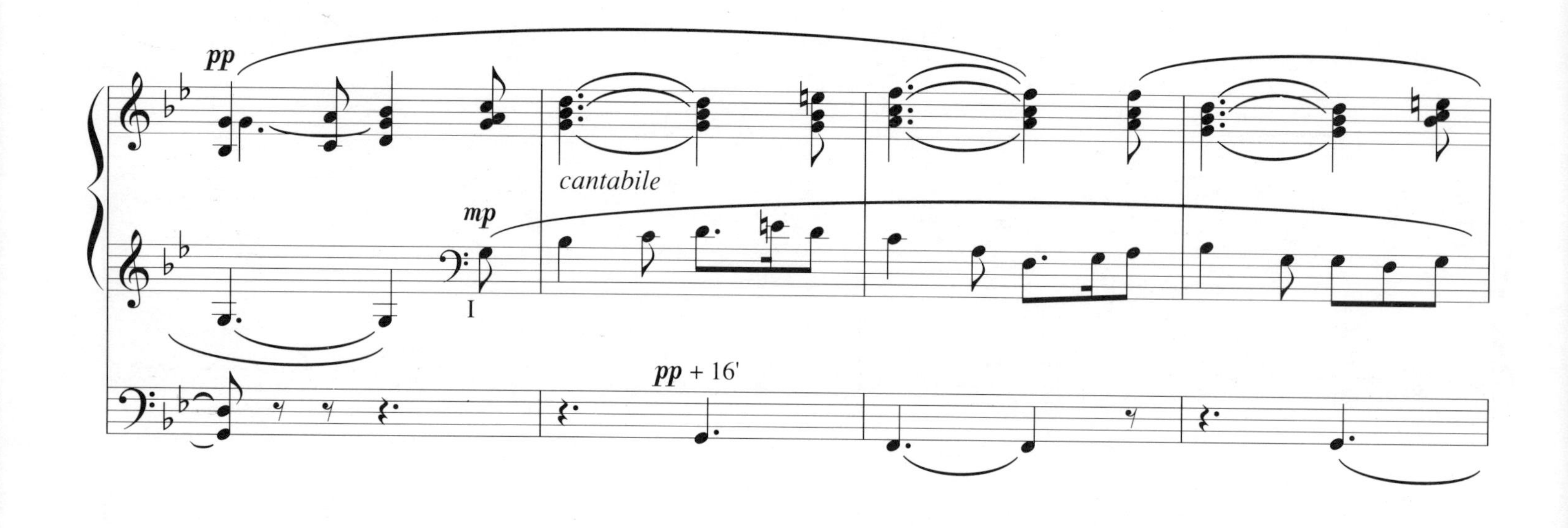

add
+ 4'
II
p

I p
(I) mp
(II)
pp
8' only
+ 16'
II
pp
I
mf

II
p
I p
rit.
pp
(II)
pp
8' only
+ 16'
+ 32'

to Wallace M. Coursen Jnr.

Prelude on 'Brother James's Air'

* Solo 8' Reed
Sw. Soft Strings 8' & 4'
Gt. Claribel or 8' Flute + Sw.
* Ch. Flutes 8' & 4' + Sw.
Ped. Soft 16' + Sw.

SEARLE WRIGHT

* The piece may be played on two manuals.

- 16'
+ Solo to Ped.
più mosso
Ch.
or
Gt.
mp
+ 16'
- Solo to Ped.
+ Ch. or Gt. to Ped.
mf
Gt.
f
dim.
(+ Gt. to Ped.)
rit.
poco a poco

Sw.
mp
- Gt. to Ped.
+ Sw. to Ped. (soft 16')
(Sw.)
p
Solo reed
mp
L.H.
rall.
perdendosi
pp
- 4'
+ Celeste
Sw.
+ 32'

Hornpipe

(from *Water Music*)

I 8' 4' 2' Mixt.
II Trumpet
III 8' 4' 2'
Ped. 16' 8', cpld. to I

G. F. HANDEL
arr. Christopher Morris

Allegro moderato

tr
Manual
I. *f*
Pedal

tr
II *f* (Tpt.)
tr

This arrangement can be played on two or three manuals. Dynamics are editorial.

III mf (I)
tr
I f
III (II)
mf
I f

II f
(Tpt.)
III (I)
mf
I f
tr
ff
tr

Prince of Denmark's March

JEREMIAH CLARKE
arr. C. H. Trevor

The original is for manuals only. This extended arrangement can be simplified and reduced to the original length by playing bars 1–8, 17–24, 1–8, 41–8, and 1–8. Alternatively, for a more full-textured version use bars 9–16, 25–40, 49–56, and 9–16.

25
tr
tr
II
32
back to start A (x1)
tr
tr
tr
tr
38
tr
/coda
I
II
44
tr
II
51
tr
D.C. al Fine
back to A & B

Trumpet Tune

HENRY PURCELL
arr. C. H. Trevor

The original is for manuals only.

I
II
tr
II
rit.
tr

Prélude

(from the *Te Deum*)

MARC-ANTOINE CHARPENTIER
arr. Christopher Morris

The dotted quavers, double dots, and semiquavers are editorial,
and represent the *notes inégales* which would have been used in Charpentier's day.

† The suspended B is in the original.

Trumpet Voluntary

(*Op. 6 No. 5*)

JOHN STANLEY
arr. David Willcocks

This arrangement can be reduced in length by omitting the repeat and observing the *D.C. ad lib.* on p. 49, finishing at the first time bar. There is no repeat in the original, which is for manuals and is mainly in two parts only (modern edition in facsimile: *John Stanley: 30 Voluntarys*, ed. Denis Vaughan, OUP).Crossed slurs and symbols in square brackets or small print are editorial.

D.C. ad lib.
tr
(tr)
(R.H.)
(L.H.)

(tr)
(L.H.)
(R.H.)
(tr)
(L.H.)
(R.H.)
(tr)
(L.H.)
tr
tr
tr
tr
tr
[poco rall.]
tr
(R.H.)
(L.H.)
tr

La Marche

G. F. HANDEL
arr. Donald Burrows

This arrangement may be played throughout with both hands on one manual (Full Organ), in which case the bracketed chords are to be omitted.

(Man.)
tr
I
(II)
tr
II
tr
tr
Man.

I
tr
II or III
Man.
tr
tr
tr
I
tr

Bridal March

(from *Lohengrin*)

RICHARD WAGNER
arr. Robert Ashfield

(Gt.)
p
- Sw. reed
+ Sw. 8', 4'
p
Sw.
Sw.
mf
p
- Gt. to Ped.
+ Sw. to Ped.
Gt.
mf
+ Gt. to Ped.
- Sw. to Ped.

f
Sw.
f
poco rit.
(Gt.)
mf

Nun Danket Alle Gott

(from Cantata No. 79)

J. S. BACH
arr. C.H. Trevor

I
II
I
II
I

II
I
II
rit.

Fanfare

WILLIAM MATHIAS
(1987)

Commissioned for the Inaugural Concert for the Christie Organ at the Memorial Hall, Barry on 28 February, 1987.

I
mf
II

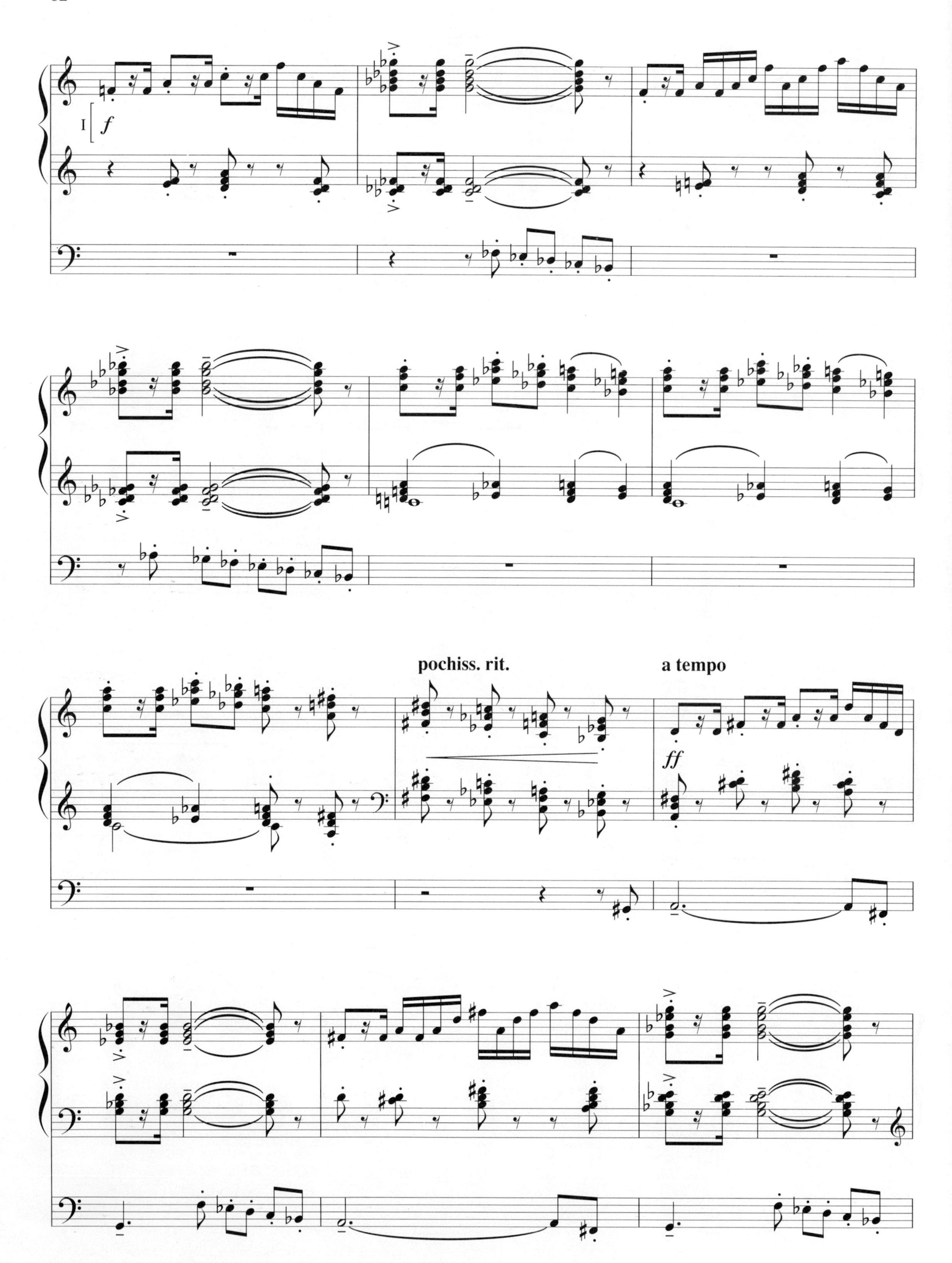
I
f
pochiss. rit.
a tempo
ff

poco rit.
a tempo
allargando
fff

March

LOUIS LEFÉBURE-WÉLY
arr. Christopher Morris

Allegro moderato

Originally for manuals only.

II
mf
I
I
f

più mosso (ad lib.)
ff
(Reed)
(I)
(Reed)
(I)

Wedding March

(from *A Midsummer Night's Dream*)

FELIX MENDELSSOHN
arr. Robert Ashfield

* All the passages marked 'Solo' are to be played wherever possible on a solo reed, either from the Solo organ or on a Gt. reed playable from the Ch. These passages are, however, so arranged that where an independent reed is not available, they may be played on the Gt. organ without any rearrangement. The Sw. to Gt. and Sw. to Pedal couplers are to be drawn throughout.

2
cresc.
ff
tr
(Gt.)
Solo
Gt.
1
2

Gt.
p
Sw.
- Gt. to Ped.
p

mp
mp
+ Full Sw.
mf
Gt.
mf
f
Solo
3
f

cresc.
ff
Gt.
ff
+ Gt. to Ped.
ff
tr
(Gt.)
Solo
Gt.
tr

tr
(Gt.)
Solo
Gt.
tr
Solo
f
- Gt. to Ped.
(Gt.)
f
Sw.
tr
f
ff

tr
Sw.
f
Gt.
f
f
+ Gt. to Ped.
1
2
tr
Solo
ff
ff
- Gt. to Ped.
f
tr
Gt.
Solo
ff
ff
Ped. stops in, cpld. to Solo
Full Organ
fff
fff

Arrival of the Queen of Sheba

(Sinfonia from *Solomon*)

G. F. HANDEL
arr. E. W. Maynard

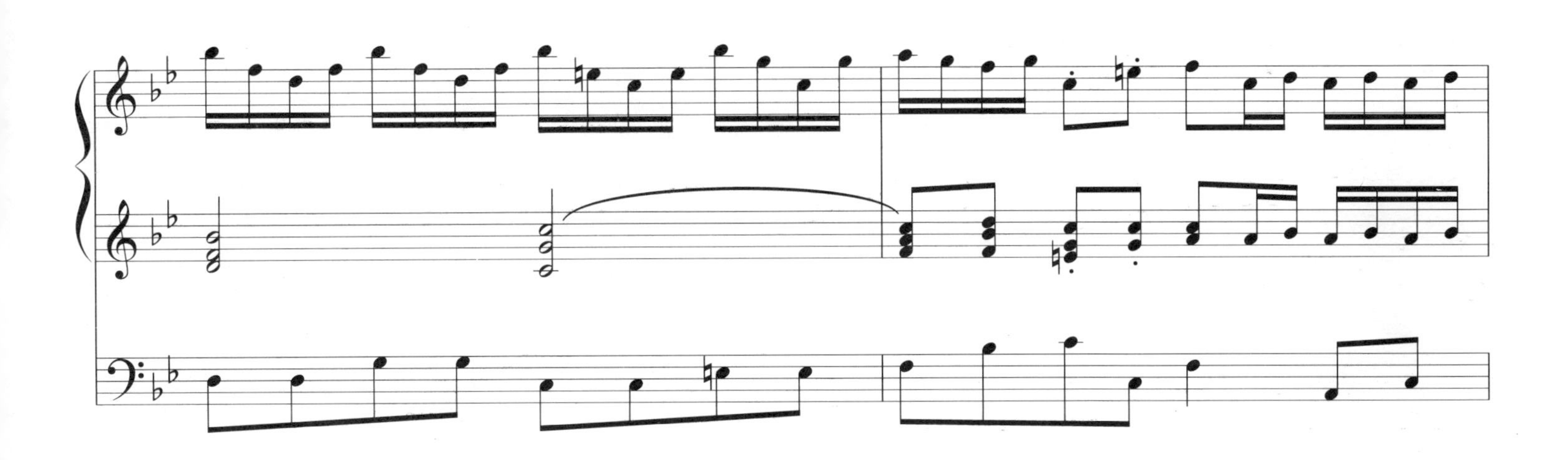

I

III (II)
I
III (II)
I

III (II)
III (II)
I
III (II)

III (II)
I
L.H.
III (II)
III (II)

I
II
(I)
II
tr
I

III (II)
I
III (II)

III (I)
II
I

rall.
tr

Grand March

(from *Aida*)

GIUSEPPE VERDI
arr. Christopher Morris

I (Tpt.)
f
II
mf

Optional cut to ⊕ (p. 88)
ff
I
mf
II
f

3
3
3
3
3
3
3
3
3
3
3

I
ff
fff

Crown Imperial

(Coronation March, 1937)

'In beawtie beryng the crone imperiall'
(William Dunbar, 1465–1520)

WILLIAM WALTON
arr. Herbert Murrill

This arrangement incorporates the cuts made by the composer in 1963. A shorter version can be played by starting from the main theme on p. 95 (fourth system), cutting back from bar 4 of p. 97 to bar 2 of p. 93, and continuing through to the end from there.

sfz
sfz
f
Ch. mf
(+ soft Sw.)

tr
tr
p
marc.
Gt.
(Ch.)
cres
cen
do
Gt.
f
Gt.
Gt. to Ped.
cres
cen
do

reduce Sw.
ff
f
+ Full Sw.

ff
Reeds
fff Reeds
f
pochiss. rall.
pochiss. meno mosso (♩= c.120)
Gt. Solo stop
mf
p
Sw.
Gt. to Ped. off
mf

poco rall.
f
a tempo poco largamente
Gt.
+ Sw.
f
Gt. to Ped.
molto marcato

rit.
Solo Reeds
a tempo primo sub.
ff
Gt.
f

3
3
+ Full Sw.

ff
Reeds
mf
cres
cen
Gt.
– do
rit.
molto
Grandioso con millanteria
ff
fff

(largamente)
molto marc.
largamente
tr
tr

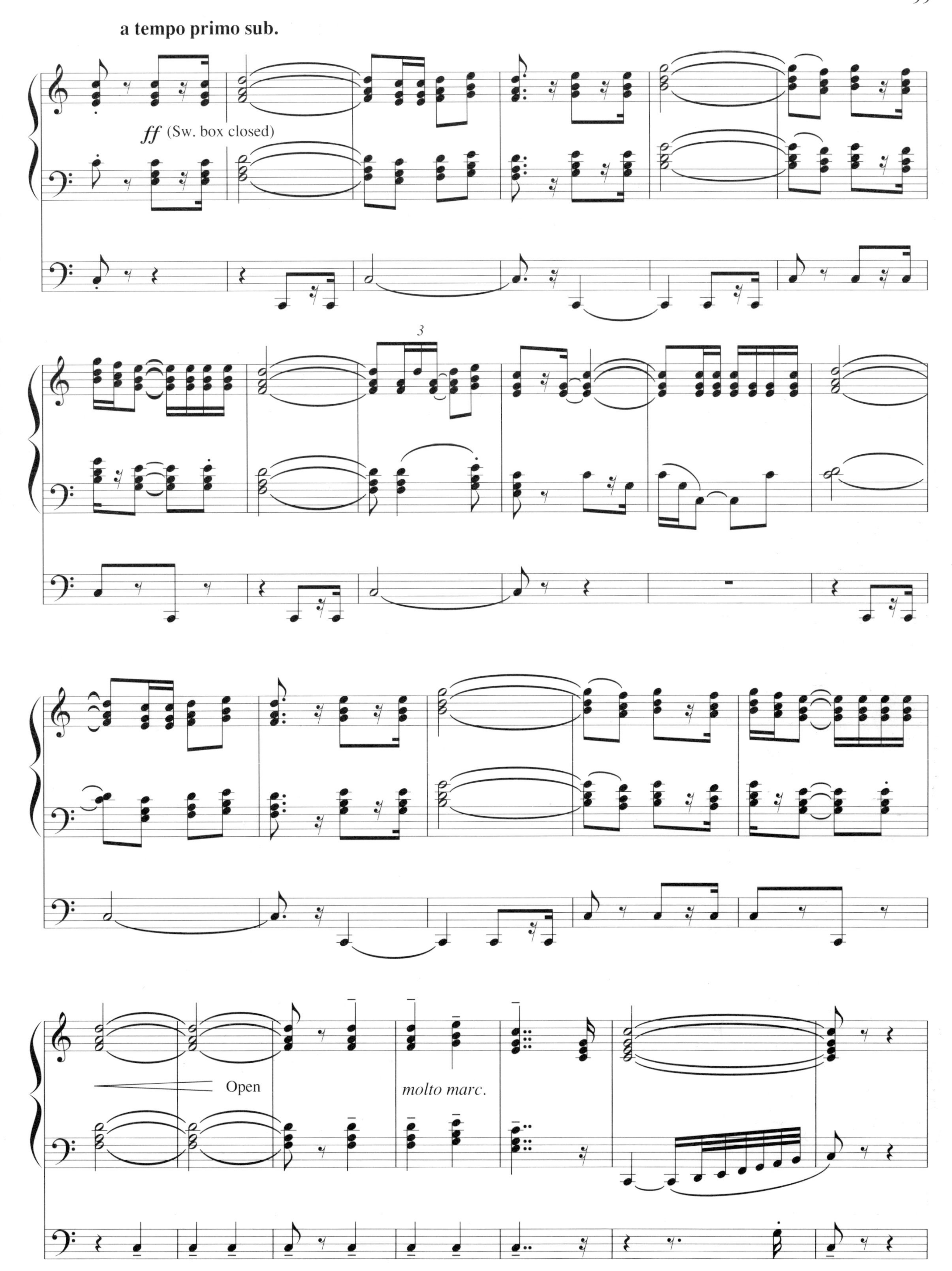
a tempo primo sub.
ff (Sw. box closed)
3
Open
molto marc.

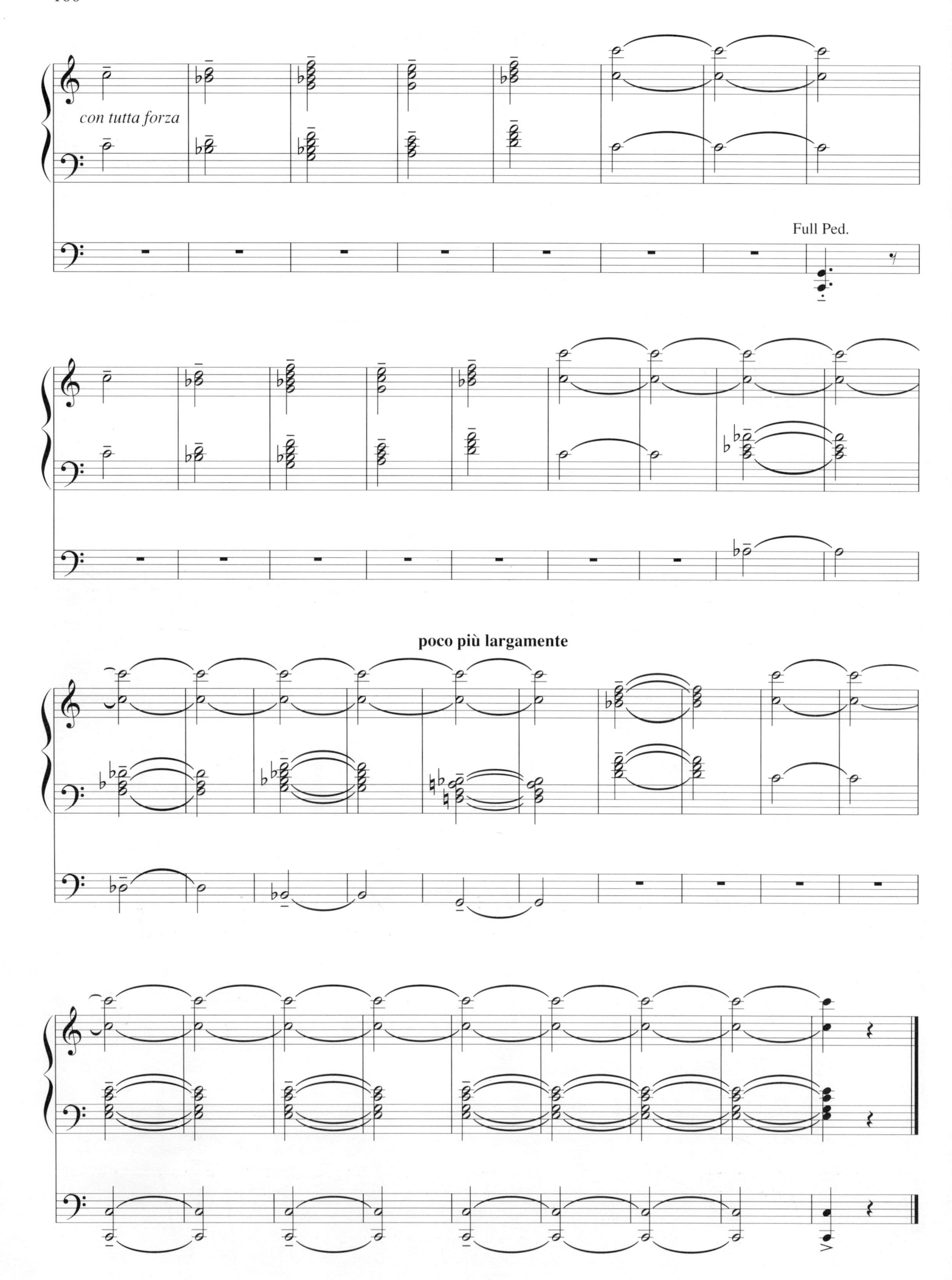
con tutta forza
Full Ped.
poco più largamente

Overture: Die Meistersinger

RICHARD WAGNER
arr. Sigfrid Karg-Elert
adapt. Christopher Morris

The tempi and dynamics are Wagner's, apart from the Italian equivalents in brackets and the final *fff* (ff). This shortened version of the overture has been adapted from Karg-Elert's arrangement *Festmusick aus den Meistersingern.*

ff
tr
Ch.
meno f
Sw.
più p
- Gt. to Ped.

dim.
Ch.
Sw.
più p
Ein wenig rallent.
(poco rall.)
Tempo
pp
cresc.
f
stacc. e
più f
Gt.
f sehr gehalten
+ Gt. to Ped.

Sehr gewichtig
(Molto pesante)
ff
più f

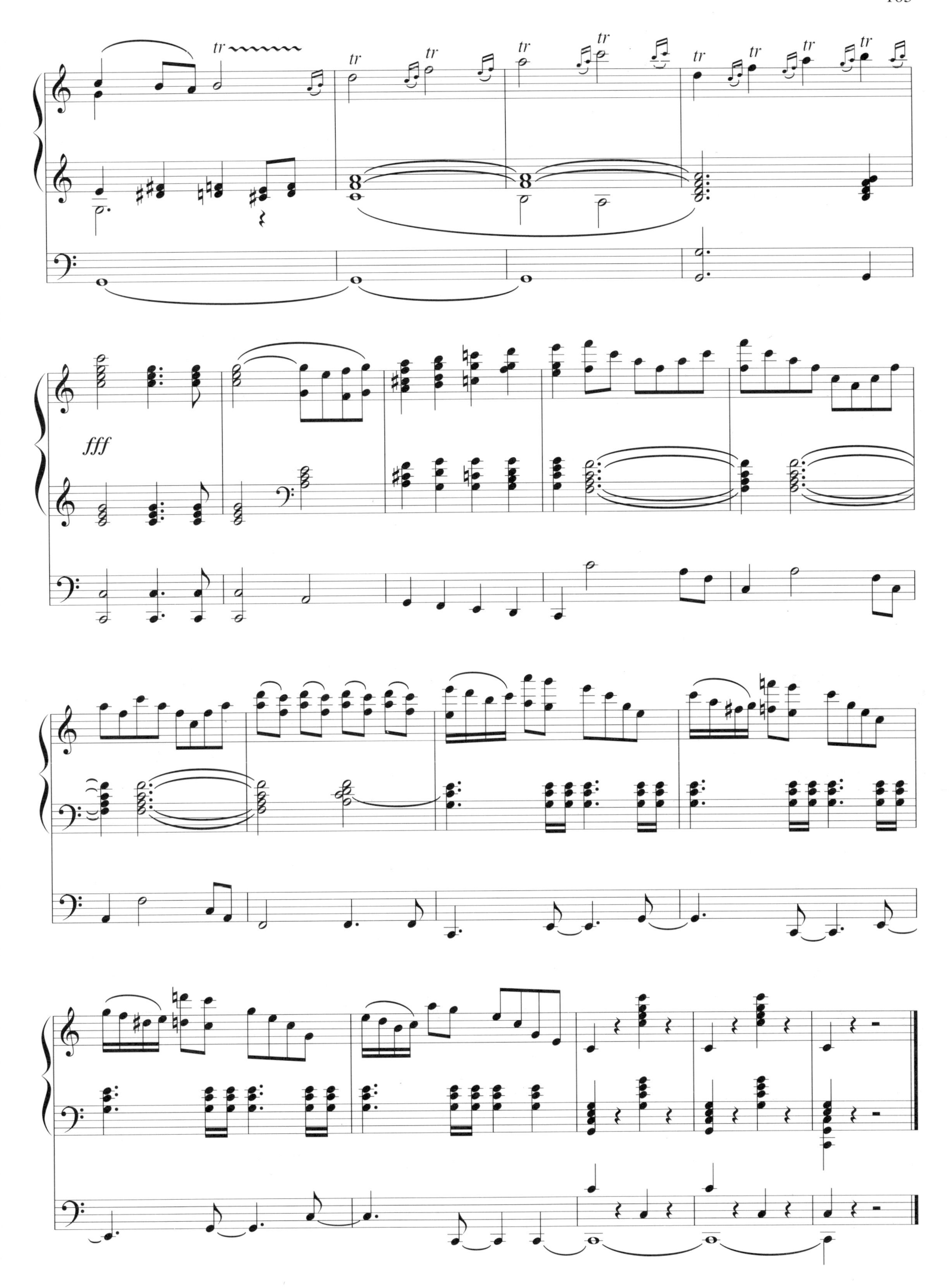
tr
fff

to Geoffrey and Pam Coffin

Trumpet Tune

ANDREW CARTER

Crisply (♩ = 70)

Manual

Gt. + Sw. *f*

Pedal

Tpt.

Sw.

poco rall.

a tempo
8va bassa (ad lib.)
(loco)
Gt.
f
molto rit.
mf
dim.
Sw.
mp
LOVE SONG
Tempo rubato
Solo 1
p
Str.

Solo 2
ten.
Solo 1
Solo 2
rall.
Solo 1
tempo primo
Tpt.
f
Sw.

poco rit.
a tempo
allarg.
a tempo
Gt.
+
Sw.
ff
+ reed
Full + Tpt.

March

HENRY PURCELL
arr. C. H. Trevor

1
2
(tr)
1
tr
2

Toccata

(from Symphonie No. 5)

CHARLES-MARIE WIDOR

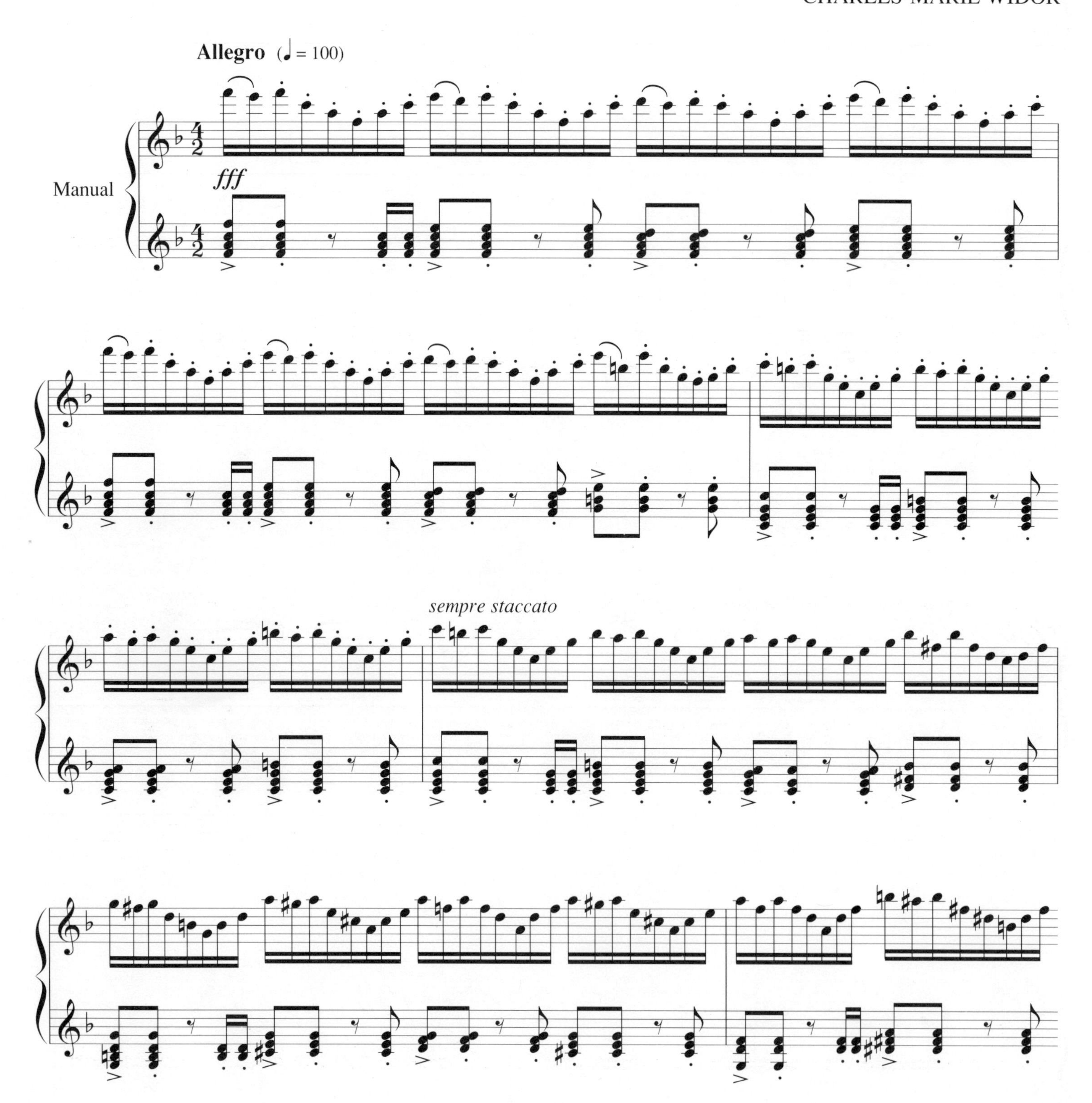

With the exception of the l.h. passage in bb. 66–74, this piece should be played on one manual, the French *Grand Orgue* (Gt.). On Widor's organ, the diminuendo in bb. 31–3 and the crescendo in bb. 42–50 would have been made by means of a series of ventil pedals controlling ranks of stops from the various manuals, which would have been coupled to the *Grand Orgue*. The marking 'R' on p. 117 indicates that at this point the performer should be playing on stops from the *Récit* (Sw.) only, coupled to the *Grand Orgue*.

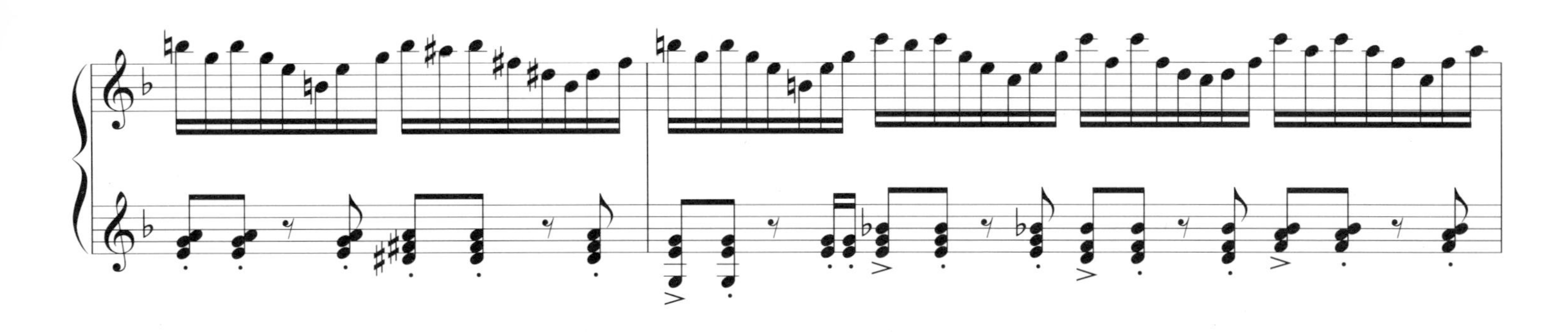

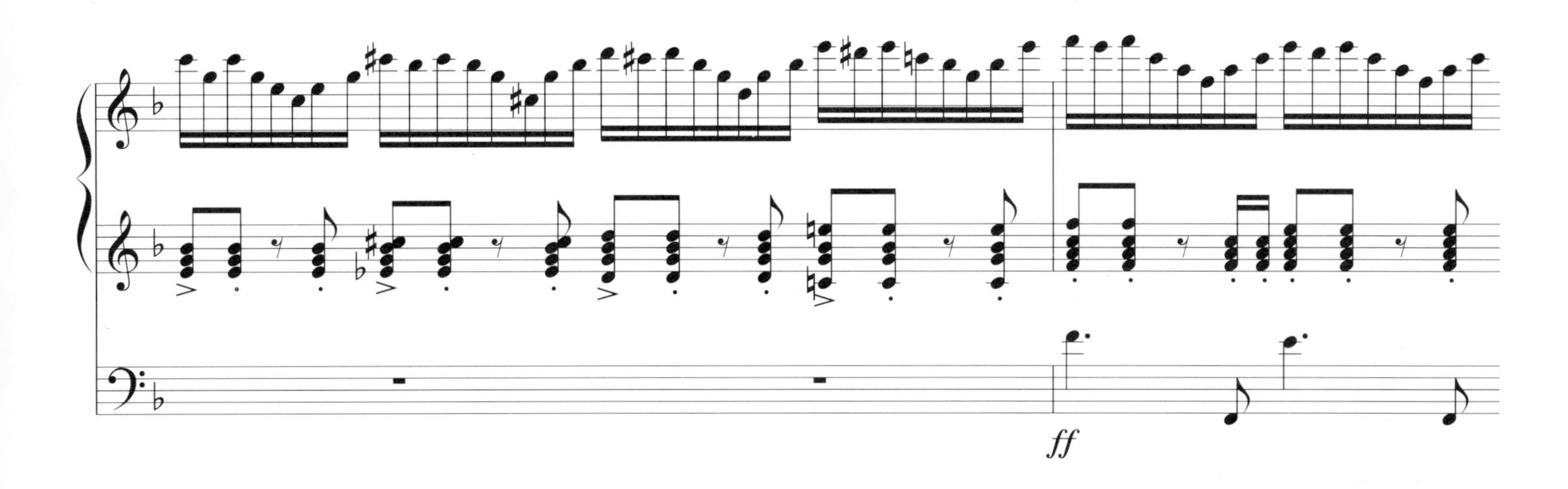
ff

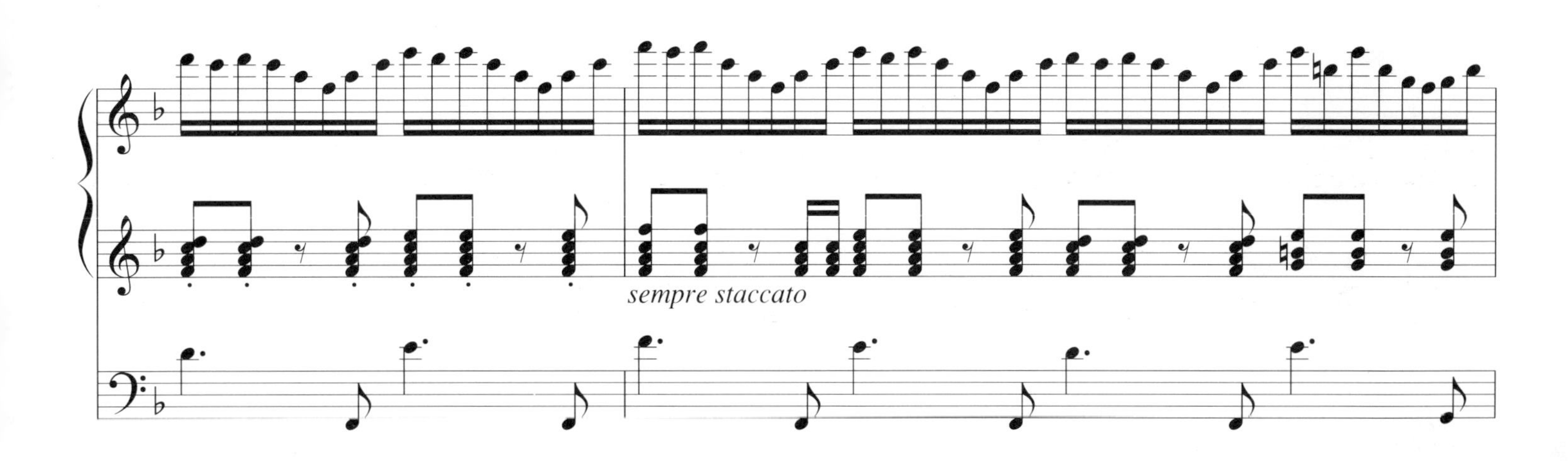
sempre staccato

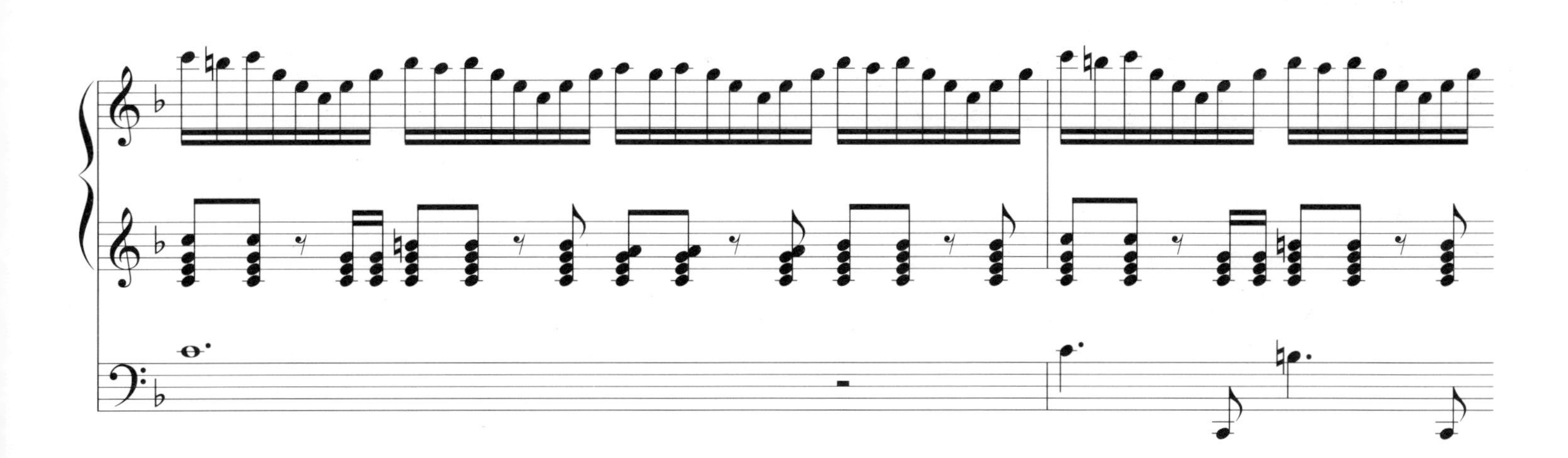

sf
sf
sf

mf
p
R
pp
cresc.

pp
cresc.
mf
cresc.
ff

f
ff
fff
fff
Maestoso
sf
sf

diminuendo
8va
PR
sempre diminuendo
8
8

8
8
cresc.
8
cresc.
fff
fff

Ouverture

(from *Fireworks Music*)

G. F. HANDEL
arr. C. H. Trevor